Howard

PUPPET STAGES AND PROPS WITH PIZAZZ

Donation

Can · Make · and · Do Books

PUPPET STAGES AND PROPS WITH PIZAZZ

53 Puppet Accessories Children Can Make and Use

by Joy Wilt

Gwen Hurn

John Hurn

Photography by John Hurn

CREATIVE RESOURCES

Waco, Texas

Acknowledgments

We wish to express our heartfelt thanks to Kathee Dayvolt for editing and Diana Crawford for typing the manuscript.

We also wish to thank our models Eric Atkinson, Stephanie Crawford, Larry Crum, Brett and Chris Noble, and David and Angie Smith for their help.

Finally, we would like to thank John Hurn for his heroic effort in the photography and lab work for this book.

Contents

IV. COSTUMES

About Puppets

A puppet is a figure of a person, animal, or object that is made to move by the efforts of a human being—child or adult. It derives its "life" and "personality" from that person's efforts and imagination.

Puppets belong in a child's world because they are
  —fun
  —educational
  —entertaining

Puppets have the potential to
  —stimulate a child's *imagination*
  —provide ways in which a child can express his *creativity*
  —assist a child in *expressing* his thoughts and feelings
  —help a child develop his *listening* and *verbal* and *language* skills
  —give a child opportunities to use and develop his *small muscles*
  —provide opportunities for *socialization* in which children are constructively planning, working, and playing together

Puppets can be used specifically
  —as an art or craft project
  —to tell or dramatize a story
  —to teach facts or concepts
  —to play musical instruments or sing songs

—to recite poems, facts, Bible verses
—to ask and/or answer questions
—to impart information
—to make announcements
—to distribute prizes
—to give directions and/or instructions
—for role playing
   etc., etc., etc.

These puppets can be made and used at
—home
—school
—church
—social functions
—recreation programs

Puppets are categorized on the basis of how they move. Generally speaking, puppets are moved by a person's fingers or hands, or by strings or rods. If a puppet is moved by a person's fingers, it is called a "finger puppet." If it is moved by a person's hand, it is called a "hand puppet," and so on. Marionettes, of course, are "string puppets." Miscellaneous puppets that do not fit into any of these categories are generally referred to as "novelty puppets."

This book, which deals with puppet stages, lighting, costumes, and props, is the third in a series of three books on Puppetry. The first one specialized in hand and finger puppets and the second in rod, string, and novelty puppets.

The puppets that we recommend are simple enough to be made by children. We believe children should not only be allowed but encouraged to make their own puppets. It is our experience that anything a child makes seems to have more meaning to him. It is our experience also that a child will find it easier to use a puppet that he has made himself; generally speaking, it is easier for a child to create a character than it is for him to adapt himself to one. Not the least important reason for children to make their own puppets is the pride and sense of satisfaction they derive from having made something themselves.

We want to emphasize that the pictures and patterns provided in this book are merely ideas and suggestions. They should be used as guidelines only. The child should be encouraged to individualize his own puppet by modifying the basic idea or pattern in any way he chooses. The important thing for the child is not to reproduce a puppet from this book but rather to create his very own puppet.

JOY WILT

Puppet
Stages

Finger-Puppet Box Stage

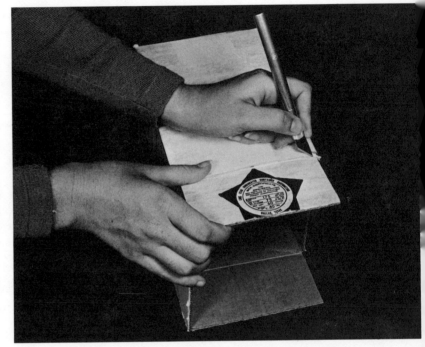

1. First, take the box and cut a window in the front, an inch from the top and sides, as shown. Also, cut out the bottom half of the back side of the box.

2. Cut off the box flaps.

You will need: Small rectangular box or shoe box
Marker
Knife
Felt, trim, etc. to decorate stage
White glue

3. Decorate the box as desired with felt, trim, or whatever else you can think of.

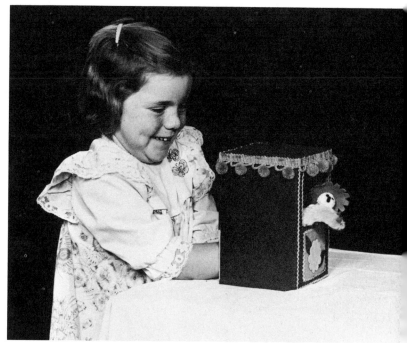

4. To use this stage for a puppet show, slide your hand with a finger puppet on it through the hole in back of the stage.

5. The puppet on your finger should show through the front window.

6. Here is a variation of the same stage,
   done in wood.

Oatmeal Carton Stage

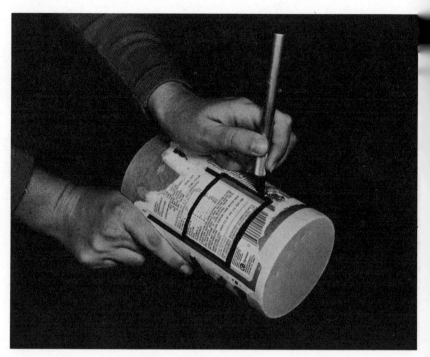

1. Remove lid from the oatmeal carton and turn carton upside down. Draw a front window about 1″ down from what is now the top of the carton. Next, draw an opening on the back side of the carton on the bottom half (there should be no bottom border).

2. With a knife or a pair of scissors, cut along the lines you have drawn.

You will need: Empty oatmeal carton
Marker
Knife or scissors
White glue

Felt, paint, trim or construction paper to decorate

3. Decorate as desired with paint, felt, construction paper, or trim.

4. Set the finished stage on a table or piano bench. Slide your hand with the finger puppets on it through the back window until the puppets show in the front window. You are now ready to begin the puppet show.

Shallow Box Stage

1. Cut a long, narrow box down to the size desired for the stage.

2. Now, decorate the box with paint or felt, as desired.

You will need: Long, narrow box
Knife
Paint or felt
White glue

Felt or fabric for
dropcloth
Tape

3. With tape, attach a piece of felt or fabric for a dropcloth (dark fabric works best; we have used light cloth in the picture to make this step clearer).

4. Place the completed stage on a table or piano bench and slip your puppet in from the back, under the dropcloth.

Two-Window Box Stage

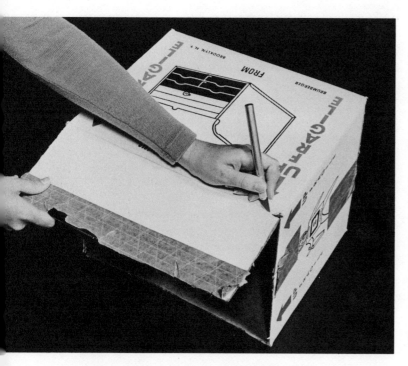

1. Cut the top flaps off the box.

2. Next, on the box bottom, cut two windows about the same size, one on top of the other.

You will need: Rectangular box
Knife
Marker
Felt, paint, or trim
White glue

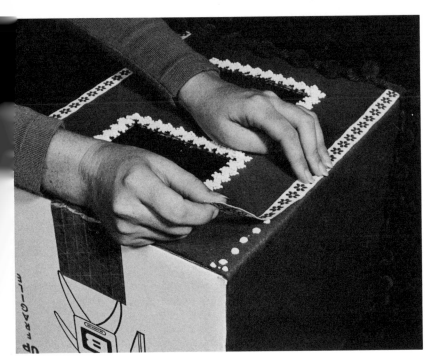

3. Decorate the box as desired with felt, paint, or trim.

4. Set the decorated stage on a table or piano bench and you are ready to begin your puppet show.

Shoebox Finger-Puppet Stage

1. Lay a shoebox on its side. Now draw a line about 2″ from all four edges of the side facing up.

2. Cut out along these lines and decorate the box as desired.

You will need: Shoebox Paint, construction
Marker paper, trim, etc.
Knife to decorate
White glue Fabric or felt for skirt
4 empty paper towel rolls Needle and thread

3. Glue a paper towel tube to each corner of the box on the side you just cut. Let the glue dry.

4. To make a stage skirt, cut a rectangle from fabric. It should be a little wider than the paper towel tubes are long, and long enough to go around three sides of the box plus about 6″.

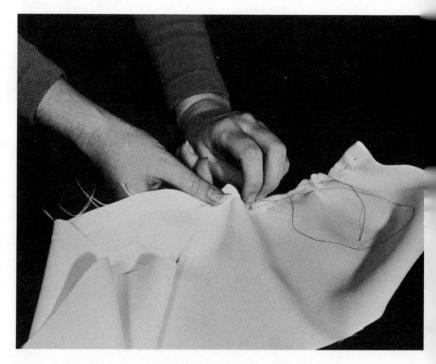

5. Fold over one of the long sides of the fabric rectangle, as shown, and sew a running stitch all along this side.

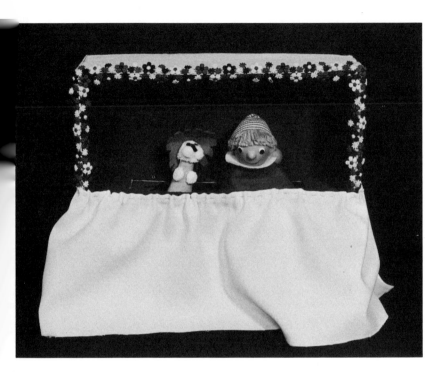

6. Gather skirt slightly by pulling the ends of the thread until skirt fits around the box as shown. Glue skirt to three sides of the stage, leaving the back open. Now the stage is ready for use.

Box Stage for Two

1. Set the box on its side with the open end toward you. Draw a rectangular slot on what is now the top of the box. The slot should be narrower than the bottoms of your puppets, and long enough to fit two puppets in comfortably.

2. Cut the slot out. Then cut the flaps off the end of the box.

You will need: Rectangular box
Marker
Knife
White glue
Felt, trim, etc. to decorate

3. Decorate the stage as you like.

4. Set the decorated box on a table or piano bench, slide the puppets through the slot, and you are ready for a story.

Traditional Box Stage

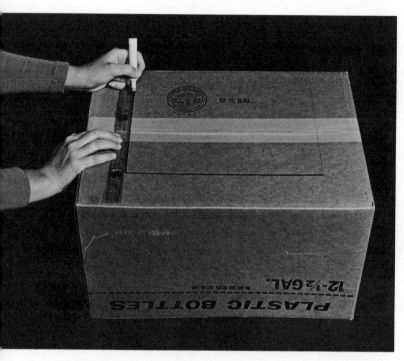

1. Take a square or slightly rectangular box, cut the top flaps off, and draw the kind of stage opening you want on the bottom of the box.

2. Cut along the drawn lines and decorate as desired.

You will need: Cardboard box
Marker
Knife
White glue

*Felt, paint, trim, etc.
to decorate*
*Felt or fabric for
dropcloth*

3. Tape a piece of felt or fabric to the back opening of the stage for a dropcloth (black cloth works best).

4. Slide the puppets between the backdrop cloth and the stage. Your show is ready to begin.

Pop-a-Puppet Stage

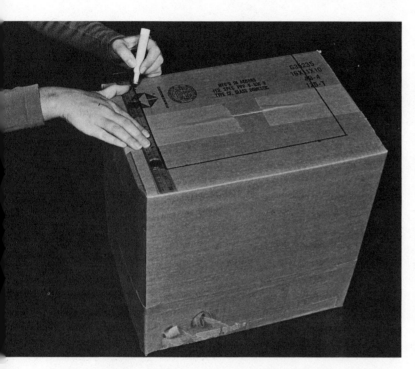

1. Take a tall, square, or rectangular box and set the open end of the box on the table or floor. Draw a pop-up lid on the edge of the box that faces up. The lid should be drawn two or three inches away from each of three edges and all the way to the edge of the fourth side, as shown.

2. Cut along the line and lift up the lid. Cut out the bottom half of the back side and cut off the box flaps.

You will need: Tall box
Marker
Knife

Felt, trim, etc.
to decorate
White glue

3. Decorate the box as desired with felt, trim, or whatever you wish.

4. Set the finished stage in the desired area. Slide the puppeteer's arm, with the puppet on it, through the back slot. Your puppet is ready to pop out and perform.

Three-Door Stage

1. Cut off the flaps and half the back side of the box.

2. Next, draw and cut out three doors on the front side of the box.

You will need: Large box
Marker
Knife

Felt, trim, etc.
to decorate
White glue

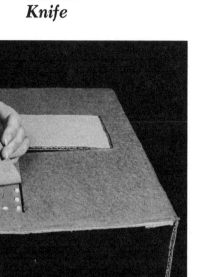

3. Decorate the box as desired.

4. Place the stage on the edge of a table or piano bench, position the puppeteers, and the show is on!

Lap Box Stage

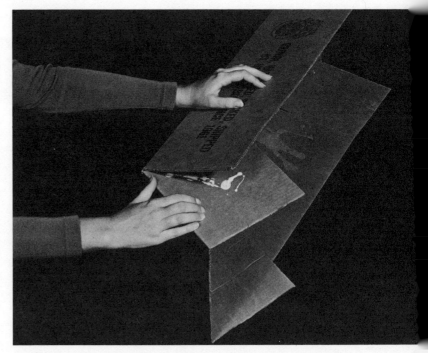

1. Cut the box in half between the two top flaps, as shown (this should loosen all the flaps).

2. Now pull the two shorter sides of one of the halves out to about a 45° angle. Glue them in place. When glue is dry, cut a stage opening in the side of the box.

You will need: *Medium sized box*   *Fabric or felt for*
                        Knife   *dropcloth*
                        White glue   *Paint, trim, etc. to*
                        Tape   *decorate*

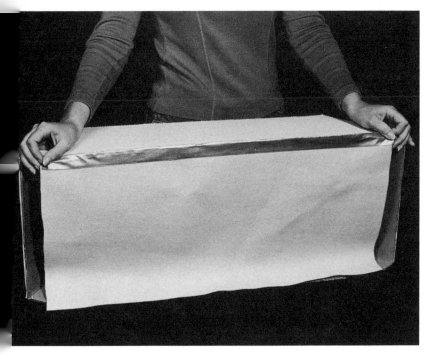

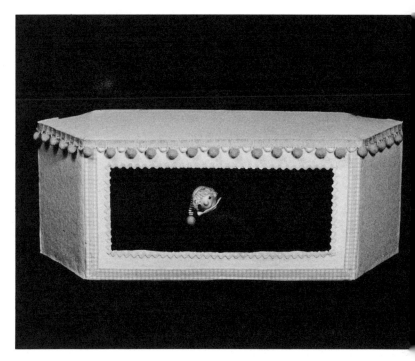

3. Decorate as desired and tape a piece of felt or fabric to the top back of the box for a dropcloth (black cloth works best).

4. Now, set the box on a chair, couch, table, or piano bench. Slide the puppets in front of the dropcloth and your play is ready to begin.

37

Flat Tray Stage

1. Cut down a square or rectangular box so that the sides are about 4″ in height.

2. Using a saucer as a guide, draw two circles, about 2″ apart, on the bottom of the box. Cut these out.

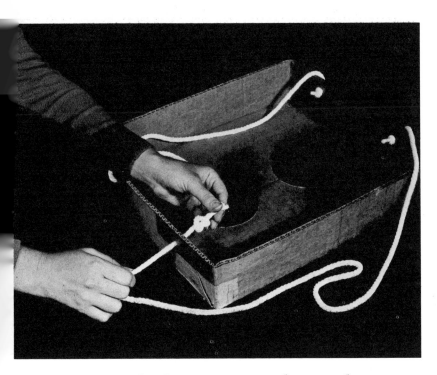

3. With the paper punch, punch two holes, approximately 3″ to 4″ apart, in each of the tray's two shorter sides. Now, tie a knot in one end of each cord. Starting from the inside of the box, put the unknotted end of each cord through the righthand hole, loop it over the top, and put it through the outside of the lefthand hole, as shown. Knot that end from the inside of the box to secure the cord.

4. Decorate the stage as desired. Now, slip the looped cords over the puppeteer's head and bring his two hands, with puppets on them, up through the holes in the bottom of the tray. Adjust the cords so that the tray is level. Your show is now ready to begin.

39

Box Stage for String Puppets

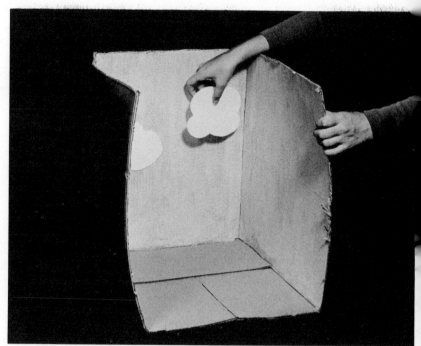

1. Cut the top flaps and one side of the box off.

2. Decorate the box as desired.

You will need: Large box   White glue
Knife   2 Chairs
Felt, paint, etc.   Gameboard stage
to decorate   (p. 44)

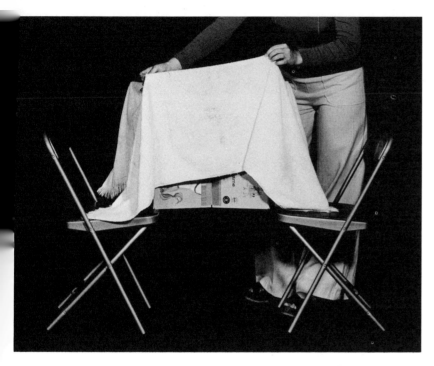 

3. Now, set up two chairs facing each other, approximately 2′ apart. Set the gameboard stage across the two chairs. If you are draping the stage, do it now.

4. Slide the stage between the chairs so the cut-out side is facing the front. Seat the puppeteers behind the gameboard stage and begin your show.

Cutting-Board Stage

1. Unfold a seamstress's cutting board and stand it up on end, bending the outer sides in such a way that the board will stand by itself, as shown.

2. A sheet or blanket may be dropped over the board, if desired, and taped in place.

You will need: *Seamstress's cutting board*
Sheet or blanket (optional)
Tape (optional)

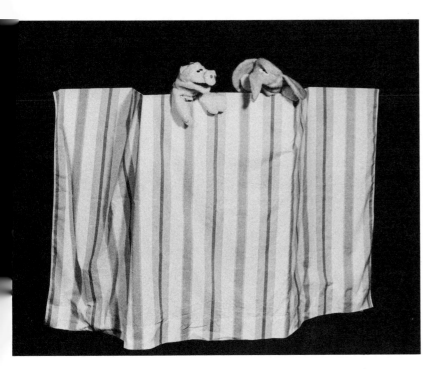

3. When the puppeteers are in place behind the stage, the play is ready to begin.

Gameboard Stage

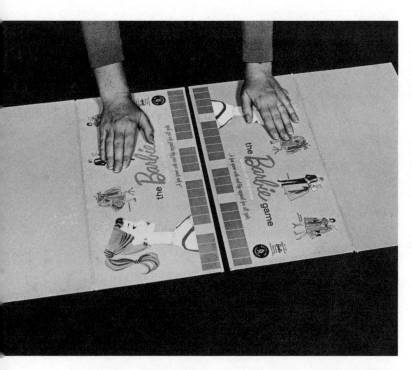

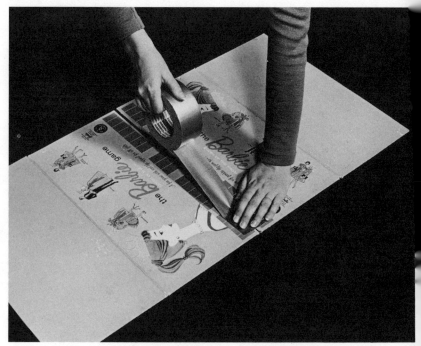

1. Pick two old gameboards and lay them, unfolded, face down side by side so that the meeting edges of the boards are parallel with the board seams.

2. Now, tape the meeting edges together to make a third seam.

You will need: 2 gameboards (same size)
Tape
Sheet or towel (optional)

3. Stand the boards on end with the two outer seams slightly bent toward the inside. The stage may now be draped with a towel or other cloth.

4. Set the stage on a table to make it ready for the puppeteers (or use with the Box Stage for String Puppets as shown on p. 40).

Shaped Cardboard Stage

1. Draw desired shape on a flat piece of cardboard and cut it out. Leave tabs on the sides, as shown, so the stage will stand up on its own.

2. Decorate as desired with paint, felt, or construction paper. Trim the bottom of the flaps at an angle as shown.

You will need: Cardboard
Marker
Knife or scissors
White glue

Paint, construction
   paper, felt to decorate
Tape

3. Bend the tabs back to the desired angle and, if needed, tape them in place.

4. This stage will now stand up on a flat surface. The stage works best when set on a table. The puppeteers kneel or stand behind it and give the show.

Blackboard Stage

1. Position the blackboard so that there is plenty of space behind it for the puppeteers.

2. A cloth covering may be draped over the board if desired.

3. Puppeteers stand behind the board and the show is on. (If the stage is tall and the puppeteers are short, they may need to stand on sturdy chairs, as shown.)

Flat Chart Stage

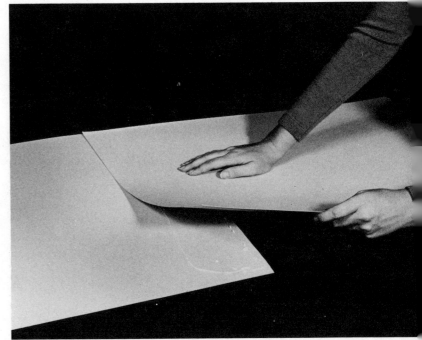

1. Draw and cut out a window in the upper third of one of the posterboards, as shown.

2. Next, glue the two sheets of posterboard together, allowing about 4″ to 6″ overlap on the shorter edge of each board.

You will need: 2 sheets of colored
                  posterboard
              Marker
              Knife or scissors
              White glue

Trim or felt
Paper punch
Cord
Chart stand or ironing
    stand.

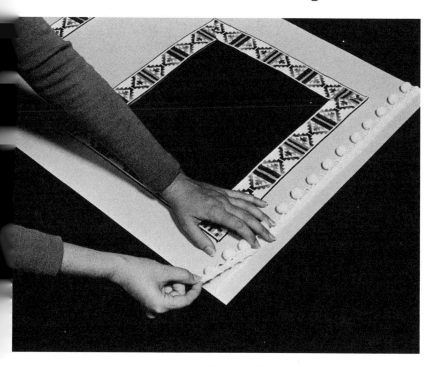

3. Decorate as desired.

4. Punch a hole near both of the top two corners and lace a 6″ to 7″ piece of cord through each hole.

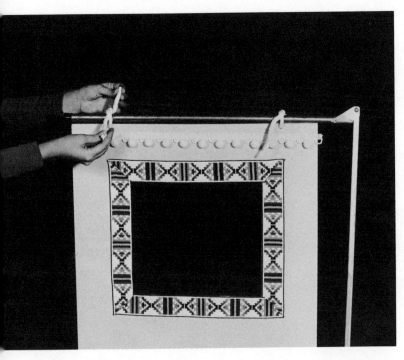

5. Tie the board to the stand, using the cords.

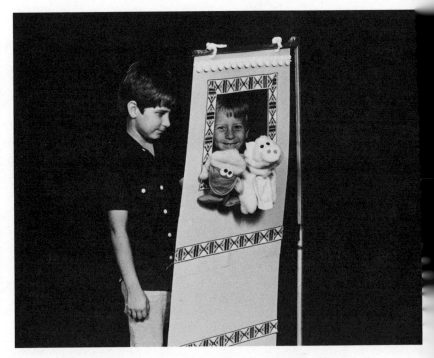

6. Place the stage in the desired area and position the puppeteers behind it.

7. The show is ready to begin.

Flat Felt Hanging Stage

1. Begin with a piece of felt about 5' x 2½'. Cut a window in the upper third, as shown.

2. Decorate as desired with pieces of felt or trim.

You will need: Felt
Scissors
Trim

White glue
2 ½" dowels
Cord

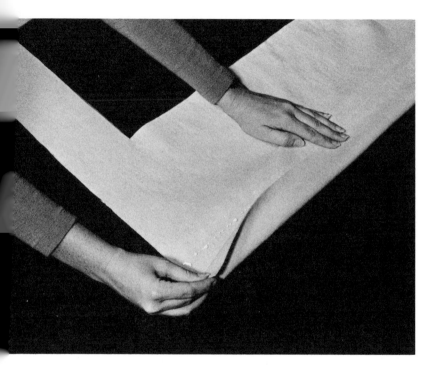

3. Fold down both ends about 2". Glue the edges to the back of the felt, as shown, so there is an open slot big enough to slide a ½" dowel through.

4. Slide a 36" dowel in each slot.

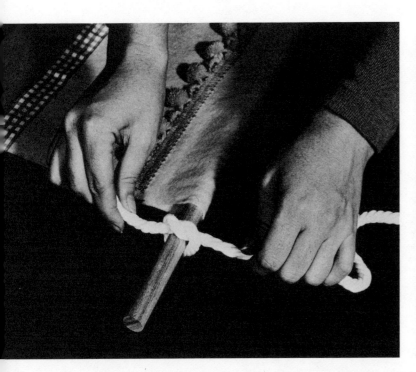

5. Take a length of cord and tie it to each end of top dowel, as shown.

6. Having hung the stage up in a suitable place (such as a doorway), position the puppeteers behind it.

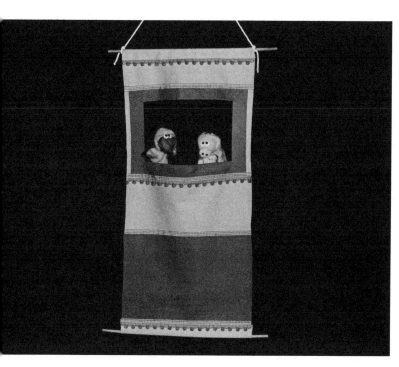

7. Ready, set, the show is on!

Open-Back Cardboard Stage

1. Draw a window in the upper third of one of the pieces of cardboard; cut it out.

2. Lay the three sheets of cardboard side by side, the windowed sheet in the middle. Tape the edges together where the pieces meet, leaving enough space between the pieces so that they can be folded either way for use or storage. Leave the outside edge of the stage untaped.

3. Decorate as desired with felt and trim.

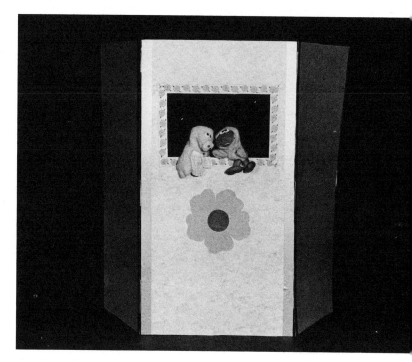

4. Stand the stage with the two end
   pieces angled back toward the puppeteers. Position the puppeteers behind it and let the show begin!

Stand-Up Stage

1. Cut a window in the upper third of one piece of cardboard (or in one side of the refrigerator box).

2. Lay all four sheets of cardboard side by side, with two solid sheets on one side of the windowed cardboard and one solid sheet on the other side. Tape the cardboard sheets together where the edges meet, leaving enough space between them so that when the sheets are taped together they can be folded either way. If you are using a refrigerator box, cut along one fold so that the sides lie like the cardboard sheets explained above.

You will need: 4 large pieces of cardboard or a refrigerator
box (can be cut down
to any size)
Knife

Duct tape
Felt, trim etc. to
decorate
White glue

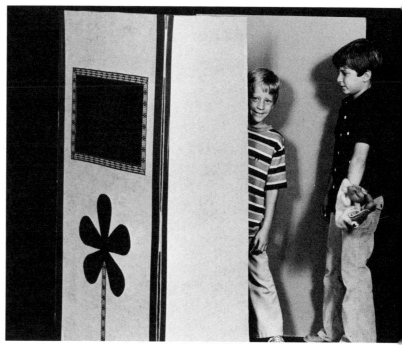

3. Decorate as desired with felt and trim
(it may be easier to decorate this stage
while it is upright).

4. Stand the stage sides in the shape of a
box with the windowed portion in
front. Place the puppeteers on the inside.

5. If desired, a cut-down piece of cardboard can be fitted to the top of the
box to make a closed-in top.

6. Bring out the puppets and start the show.

Windowsill Stage

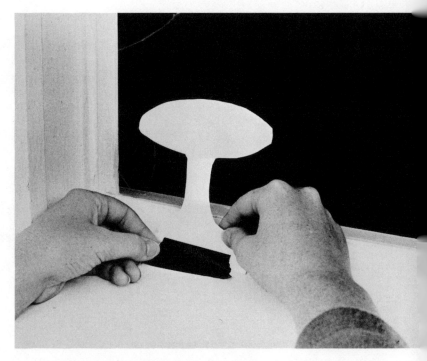

1. Decorate the windowsill with tagboard props.

You will need: Windowsill
Tagboard props (see p. 94)
Tape

2. The puppeteers perform on one side of the window while the audience views from the other.

Curtain Doorway Stage

1. Slide a curtain rod through the rod casing in the curtain and then tape one end of the rod to each side of the doorway.

You will need: Any length window curtain, 30" or more wide
Curtain rod
Tape

2. Position the puppeteers behind the curtain and all is ready for a show.

Folding-Table Doorway Stage

1. Place the table on its side and pull out the four legs for support. The top of the table should be against the doorway facing the audience.

You will need: *Average-sized card table*
Sheet or blanket (optional)

2. The puppeteers should be positioned behind the table. If you wish, you may drape the table with a sheet or blanket.

Towel Doorway Stage

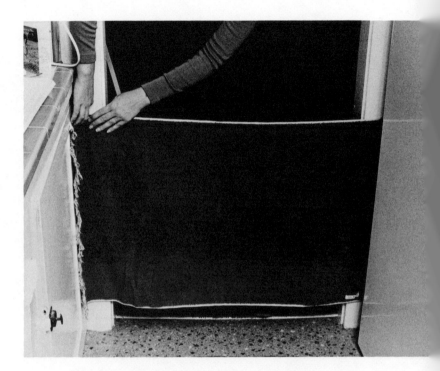

1. Tack each of the top two corners of a towel to either side of a doorway.

You will need: *Towel*
Tacks

2. The puppeteers operate their puppets from behind the towel.

Apron Stage

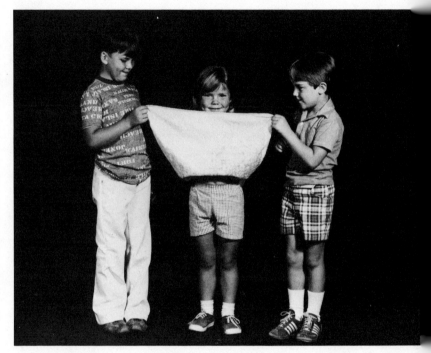

1. Tie an apron or towel snugly to the waist of one puppeteer.

2. Place a puppeteer on each side of this puppeteer, standing fairly close. Have the outer puppeteers grasp the two bottom corners of the apron with their outside hands and pull it up until it hides the head of the center puppeteer.

3. Put a puppet on one or both hands of
   the center puppeteer and a puppet on
   the inside hand of the two side puppeteers. Have them raise their puppets
   above the apron to give their show.

Folding-Chair Stage

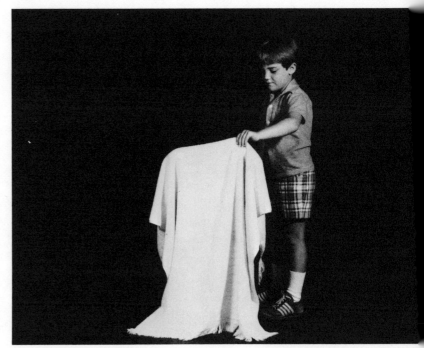

1. Place a chair with its back facing the audience.

2. Drape the towel or sheet over the back side of the chair so the legs of the chair are covered.

You will need: *Folding chair*
Sheet, towel, or blanket

3. The puppeteer places himself on his knees behind the stage (actually the front of the chair) and performs with his puppets peering over the top of the chair.

Easel Stage

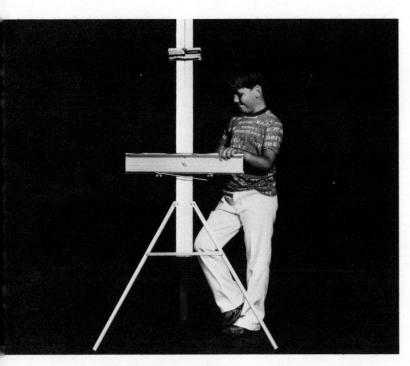

1. Set up the easel in the area where the play will take place.

2. Prop a piece of cardboard in place on the easel at a height appropriate for the puppeteers.

You will need: *Any kind of easel*
Cardboard or other kind of board
Blanket or sheet

3. Drape a sheet or blanket over the cardboard so the upper clamp of the easel holds both the blanket and the cardboard firmly in place.

4. Puppeteers stand behind the easel to put on their show.

Table Stage I

1. Place a folding table on its side and pull out all four legs.

2. Drape a sheet over what is now the three front sides. Tape the sheet to the table to hold it in place.

You will need: Folding table
Sheet or towel
Tape

3. The puppeteers, hidden on three sides
   by the sheet, make their puppets perform along the top edge of the table.

Table Stage II

1. Set up a folding table in the usual way.

2. Drap a sheet over the table top so it hangs to the floor on all sides.

You will need: Folding table
Sheet or towels
Tape

3. Position the puppeteers behind the covered table on their knees and the show is ready to begin.

Lighting

Troublelight

You will need:

Troublelight
Puppets
Puppet Stage and
  props

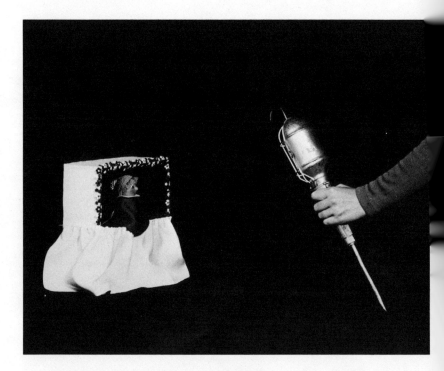

Hold or hang the troublelight in front of
the stage, approximately three feet away
from it.

Flashlight

You will need:

Large flashlight
Puppets
Puppet stage and
props

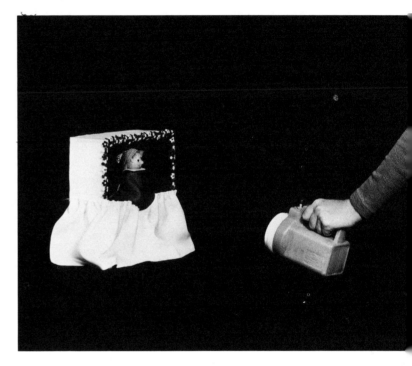

Hold or prop a large flashlight about two or three feet away from the stage front and then turn it on.

Slide Projector

Slide Projector
Small Table
Puppets
Puppet stage and
*   props*

Set a slide projector either on the same table as the stage or on a small table close to the stage. Plug it in, aim the light, and your stage is ready.

House Lamp

You will need:

House lamp
Puppets
Puppet stage and
props

Set a lamp on the same table as the stage. Move the shade until it is at the correct angle to hit the stage opening. Then, plug it in and adjust it.

High Intensity Lamp

You will need:

High intensity lamp
Puppets
Puppet stage and
   props

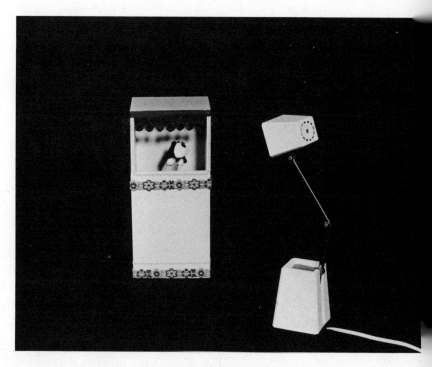

Set a high intensity lamp on the same
table as the stage and adjust it until it is
at the correct angle to light the stage
opening. Plug it in and your stage is ready
to use.

Props

Slot Props

1. Draw the desired shapes on a piece of tagboard, leaving a 1″ x 1″ tab at the bottom of each prop. (Props should be scaled to fit the size of the puppet.)

2. Cut out the props, including the tab, and decorate as desired.

3. Now, slide the tabs into slots cut in the stage, as shown. This allows the props to stand upright.

4. The show can take place between the props or in front of them.

Tape-Up Props

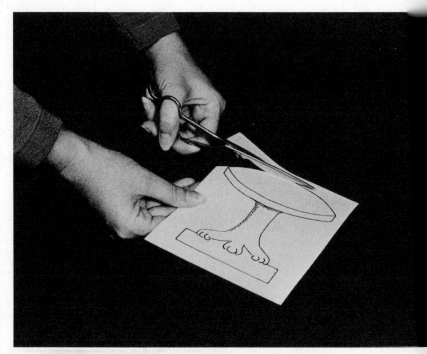

1. Draw the desired shapes on a piece of tagboard (scale the drawings to fit the size of the puppets).

2. Now, cut out the shapes and decorate the tagboard as desired.

You will need: Tagboard
Markers
Scissors
Tape

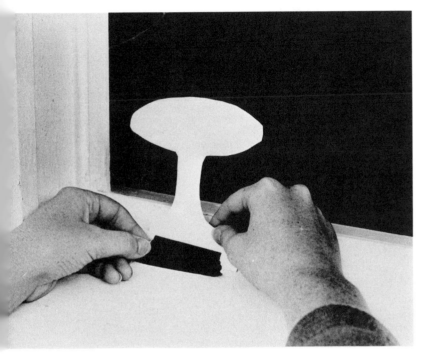

3. Tape the prop to the back side of the windowsill or to a table.

4. Place the puppeteers behind the stage and start the show.

Stand-Up Props

1. Fold a piece of tagboard or construction paper in half so that one half of the paper or tagboard is big enough for the desired prop.

2. Draw an appropriate shape and cut it out, leaving the two halves connected in a small place at the top fold.

You will need: Tagboard or construction paper
Markers

Felt
White glue
Scissors

3. Decorate the prop with felt pieces and position it on the stage.

4. The show can take place in front of, behind, or beside the prop.

Rod Props

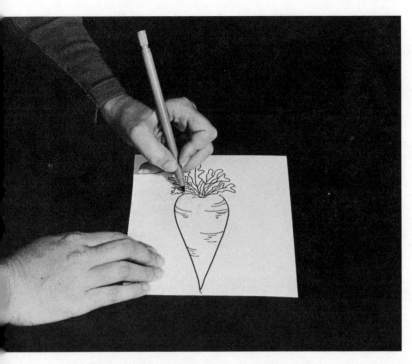

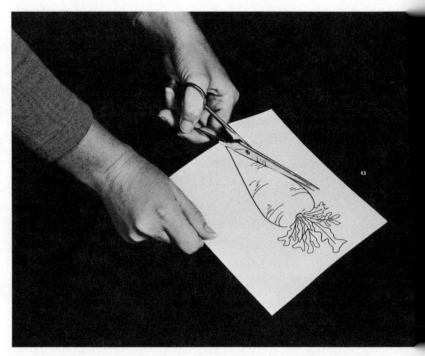

1. Draw the shape desired on a piece of tagboard.

2. Cut out the shape and decorate it with markers or felt.

You will need: Tagboard
Markers
Scissors
Felt

White glue
Wood stick (¾" screen
molding works well)

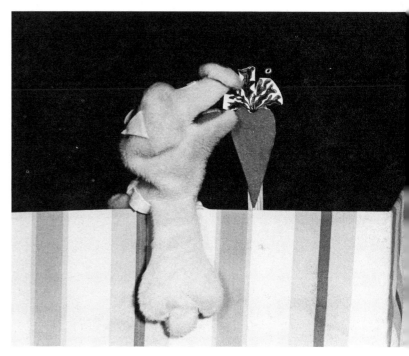

3. Glue a stick about 7" long to the back side of the prop.

4. Hold the prop by the stick, so that only the tagboard front shows.

Flap Props

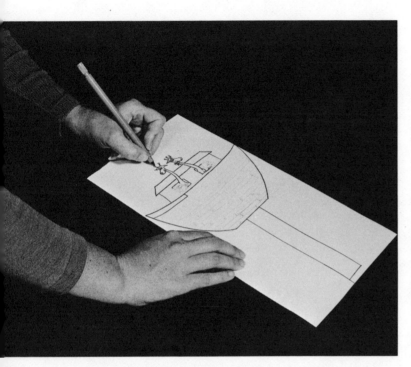

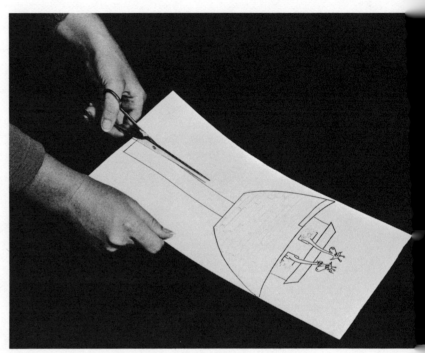

1. Draw the desired shapes on tagboard. The shape drawn should include a 1″ tab at the bottom, the same length as the prop.

2. Cut out the prop and tab and decorate as desired.

3. Bend the tab back at the base of the prop until it is perpendicular to the prop. Now, fold the end of the tab back on itself to meet the base of the prop. Take the unconnected edge of the tab and move it upward until it acts as a back brace for the prop.

4. The show can take place behind, beside, or in front of the prop.

Hanging Props

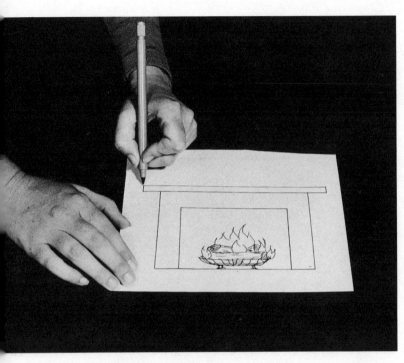

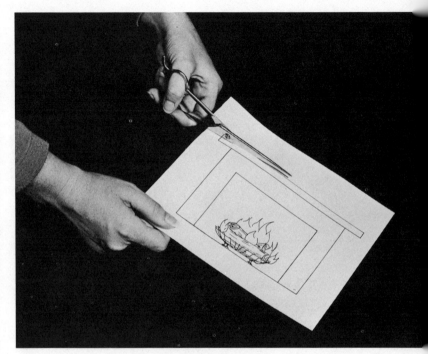

1. Draw the desired shapes on a piece of tagboard (scale the props to fit the size of the puppets).

2. Next, cut out the props and decorate them with felt and markers.

You will need: Tagboard   White glue
                               Markers   String
                               Scissors   Tape
                               Felt

3. Cut a string the same length as from the top of the stage to the top of the prop. Tape a string to the top of the prop and to the top of the stage.

4. Now, place the puppet beside the prop and the show is ready to begin.

Costumes

Hankie Blouse

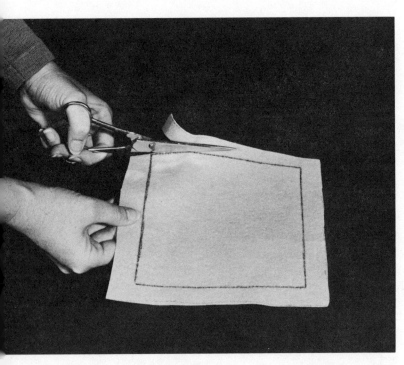

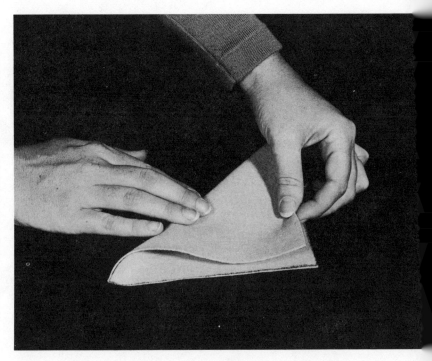

1. Draw a 6″ x 6″ square on a piece of felt and cut it out.

2. Now, take one corner of the felt square and fold it to the opposite diagonal corner.

3. Cut a neck hole in the center of the felt, big enough to allow the blouse to slide over the puppet's head. Decorate the blouse as desired.

4. Slide the blouse over the puppet's head and the puppet is dressed for the show.

Sandwich Dress

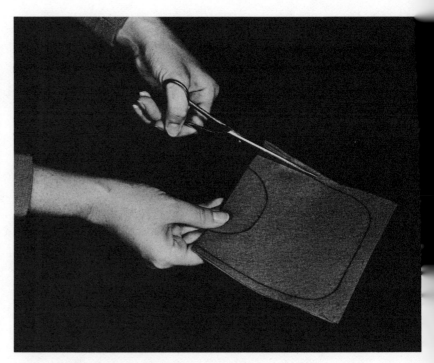

1. Fold a piece of felt. Place the top of pattern 1 (p. 141) at the fold and trace around the outside of the pattern with a marker, as shown.

2. Cut out along the traced lines, leaving the straps uncut.

You will need: *Felt*
Marker
Scissors
White glue

3. Decorate the felt to fit the puppet's role in the play.

4. Slide the dress over the puppet's head and the puppet is ready for action.

Foldover Dress

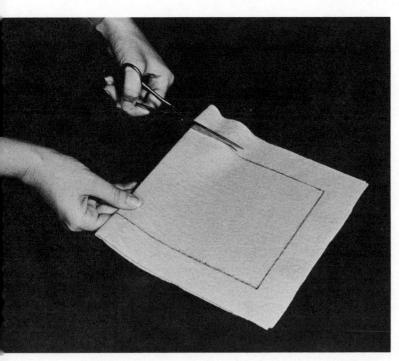

1. Draw a 6″ x 7″ rectangle on a folded piece of felt (one of the 6″ sides should be on the fold). Cut out, leaving the folded edge uncut.

2. Next, cut a V-neck in the center of the fold, as shown.

You will need: Felt
Marker
Scissors
White glue
Rickrack for trim

3. Glue the two 7″ sides together, leaving enough open space at the top of the seams for armholes and enough space at the bottom for kick pleats. Decorate the felt as desired.

4. Slide the finished dress over the puppet's head and pull the arms through the armholes. Now your puppet is dressed and ready for the show.

Drawstring Cape

1. Cut a 12″ x 6″ rectangle out of the fabric.

2. Fold and press the top edge of the cloth down approximately ½″.

You will need: Fabric   Safety pin
                               Scissors   Trim, rickrack, etc.
                               Needle and thread   White glue
                               Thick yarn or cord

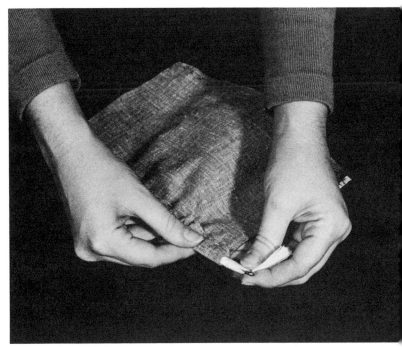

3. Now, sew the folded edge to the back of the fabric, as shown. This will form a drawstring casing.

4. Pull the cord through the casing (use a safety pin to guide the cord through the slot).

113

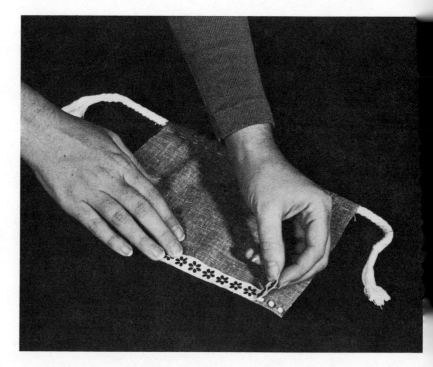

5. Decorate the cloth as desired with trim, rickrack, etc.

6. Tie the cape around the puppet's neck
   and the puppet is dressed for the show.

Tube Skirt

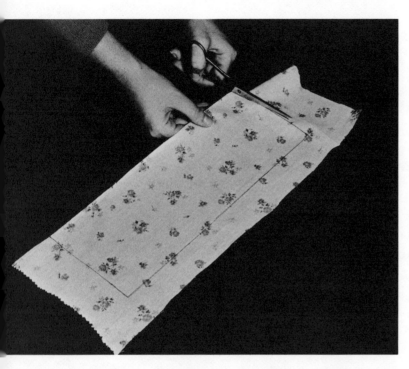

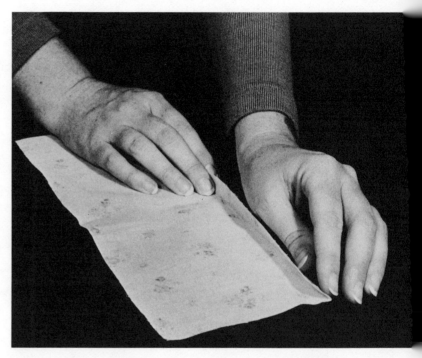

1. Cut a 6″ x 14″ rectangle out of the fabric.

2. Fold and press one of the longer edges down about 12″.

You will need:

Fabric
Scissors
Needle and thread
Elastic

Safety pin
Trim, rickrack, etc.
White glue

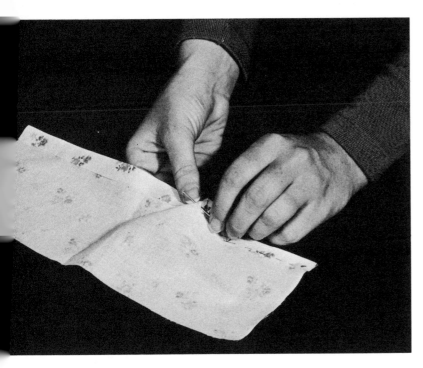

3. Hand-stitch the folded edge to the cloth in back of it, as shown. This will form a casing for the elastic.

4. Cut a piece of elastic the approximate size of the puppet's waist. Use a safety pin to guide it through the casing, gathering fabric as you go.

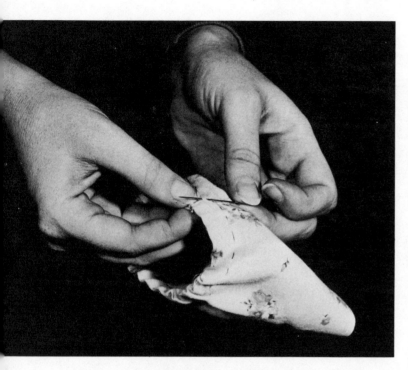

5. Secure the elastic to the cloth on both ends with needle and thread.

6. Next, glue the back seam halfway down.

118

7. Let dry and decorate with trim, rick-rack, or whatever you wish.

8. Slide the skirt down over the puppet's head to its waist. The puppet is dressed and ready for a show.

Robin Hood Hat

1. On a piece of felt, trace around the quarter-circle pattern (pattern 2, p. 141).

2. Cut along the lines you have traced.

You will need: Felt
Marker
Scissors
White glue

3. Shape the hat as shown and press it. Glue on a felt feather.

4. Place the hat on the puppet's head, and Robin Hood is ready to go!

Bonnet

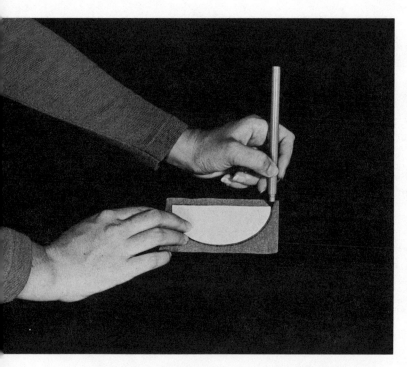

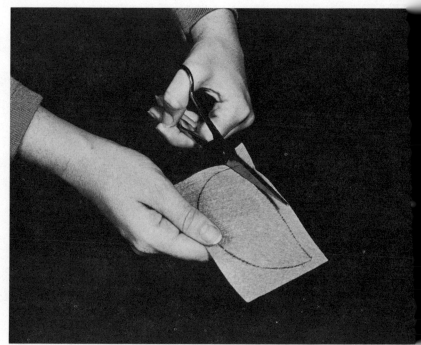

1. On a piece of felt, trace around pattern 3 (p. 141). This half-circle can be adjusted to fit any size puppet.

2. Cut the half-circle out.

You will need: Felt   White glue
                    Marker   Rickrack
                    Scissors   Lace or other trim

3. Glue a length of rickrack onto the half-circle about ¼″ from the edge of the straight side (the rickrack should extend about 2″ past the edge of the half-circle on both sides, as shown). Decorate bonnet as desired.

4. The rickrack bonnet straps are tied under the puppet's chin to hold the bonnet in place.

Collar

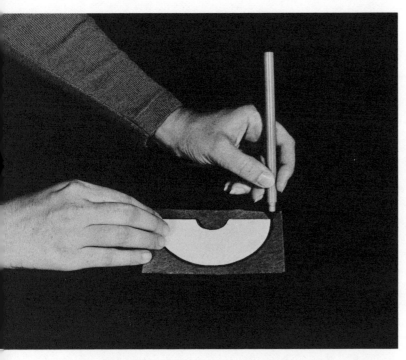 

1. On a piece of colored felt, trace around pattern 4 (p. 141). This half-circle can be adjusted to fit any size puppet.

2. Cut out along the lines you have drawn. Make the neck notch big enough to fit comfortably around the puppet's neck.

You will need: Felt
Marker
Scissors
Rickrack
White glue

3. Glue the rickrack around the neckline, leaving about 2″ extra at each end.

4. Tie the collar to the puppet's neck with the rickrack.

Clown Hat

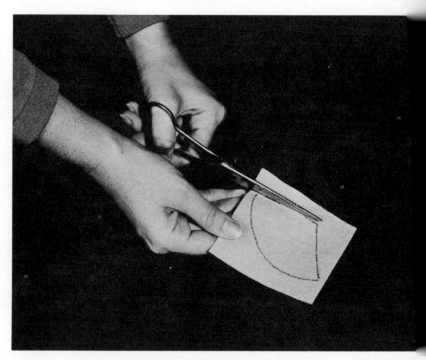

1. Using pattern 5 (p. 143), trace a two-thirds circle on a piece of colored felt.

2. Cut out along the traced lines.

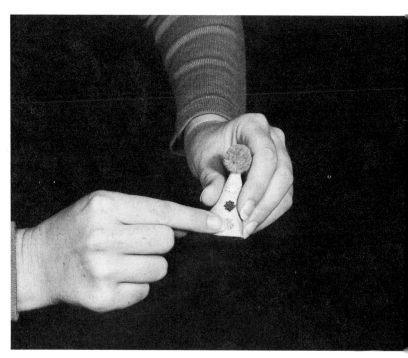

3. Bring the two edges of the circle together, as shown, and glue them.

4. Decorate the hat as desired.

5. Place the clown hat firmly on the puppet's head and it is ready to go.

6. The bottom edge of this hat can be turned up for a different look, if you wish.

Granny Hat

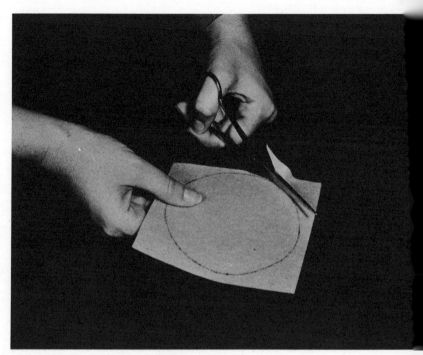

1. On a piece of felt or cloth, trace around pattern 6 (p. 143). This circle can be adjusted to fit any size puppet's head.

2. Cut out the felt circle.

You will need: *Cloth or felt*
Marker
Scissors
Needle and thread

 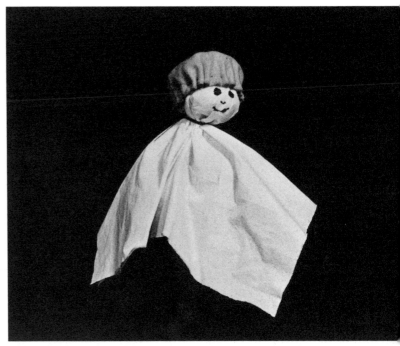

3. With a needle and thread, sew around the circle ¼″ from the edge, leaving a small gap unstitched. Now, pull one end of the thread tight and move the fabric evenly along the thread to form gathers. When the hat is small enough to fit around the puppet's head snugly, knot the ends of the thread together.

4. Place the hat on the puppet's head. This gives a special "granny look" to your puppet.

131

Cloak

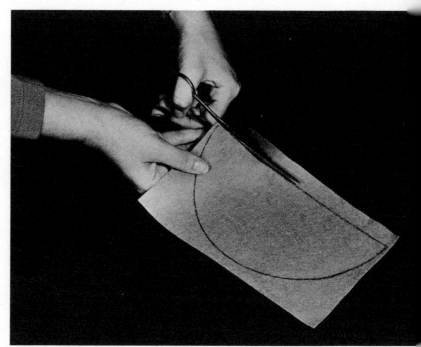

1. On a piece of felt or cloth trace around pattern 7 (p. 143). This half-circle can be adjusted to fit any size puppet.

2. Cut out along the lines you have drawn.

You will need: Felt or cloth
Marker
Scissors
Small safety pin
Yarn or rickrack

3. Drape the cloak over the puppet's head with the straight edge forward, and pin the edges together with a safety pin.

4. Now, tie a small piece of yarn or rickrack to the safety pin and tie it in a bow. The cloak is ready for Little Red Riding Hood.

Cape with Hood

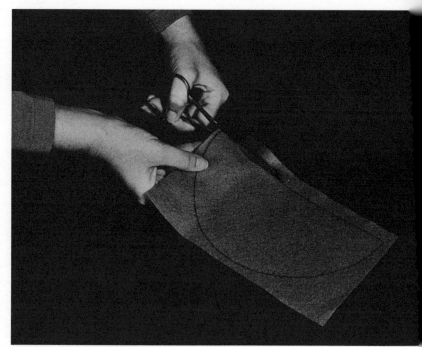

1. On a piece of felt, trace around pattern 7 (p. 143).

2. Cut the half-circle out.

3. Place the flat side of the half circle around the puppet's face. Slide a rubber band over the puppet's head and down onto its neck.

4. Tie a piece of rickrack around the puppet's neck to hide the rubber band and the puppet is ready for the show.

Hats and Masks
You Can Buy

1. *Hats:* Here are samples of different kinds of doll hats that can be purchased to add to your costumes. You can make your own hats from felt and tagboard.

2. *Masks:* This sample is a common one used extensively in puppet shows. You can make your own, or something similar, from tagboard or paper mache.

About the patterns

In the following pages you will find patterns you will need for making some of the puppets in this book. We have used one side of the page only for printing the patterns so you can cut them out if you wish. We suggest that you make tagboard duplicates of the patterns so that they will last through repeated use. If you cut the patterns from this book, you may either trace the outlines onto the tagboard and cut them out, or glue the patterns onto the tagboard and cut around them. If you wish to leave the patterns in the book, use tracing paper to copy the outlines; then proceed as above.

Remember, you can create your own pattern variations and make tagboard duplicates for them also.

Pattern	Page	Needed for
1	141	Sandwich Dress
2	141	Robin Hood Hat
3	141	Bonnet
4	141	Collar
5	143	Clown Hat
6	143	Granny Hat
7	143	Cloak
		Cape with Hood

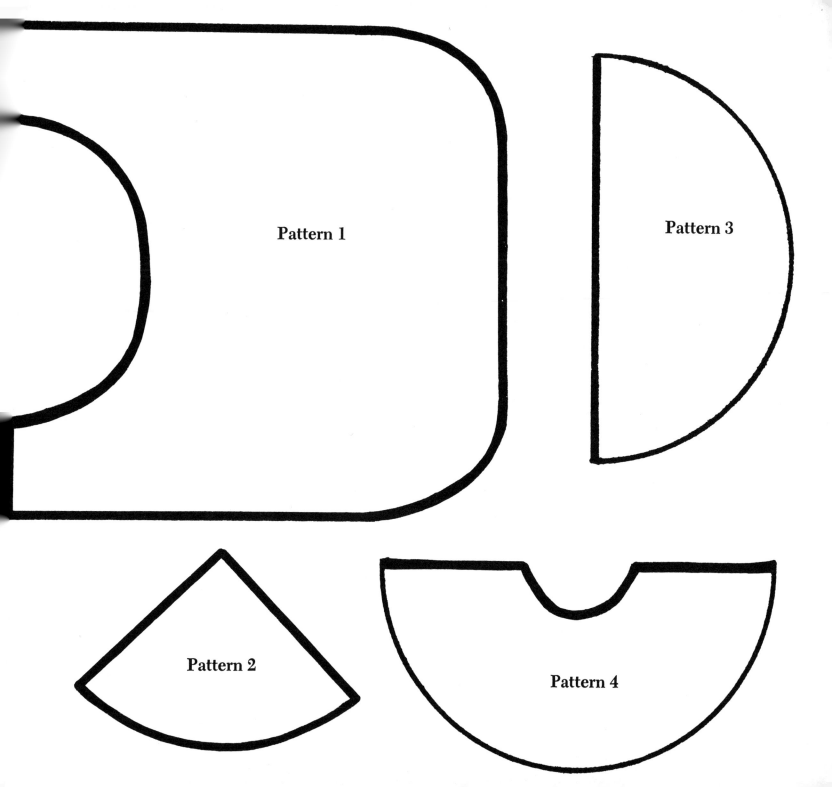

Pattern 1

Pattern 3

Pattern 2

Pattern 4

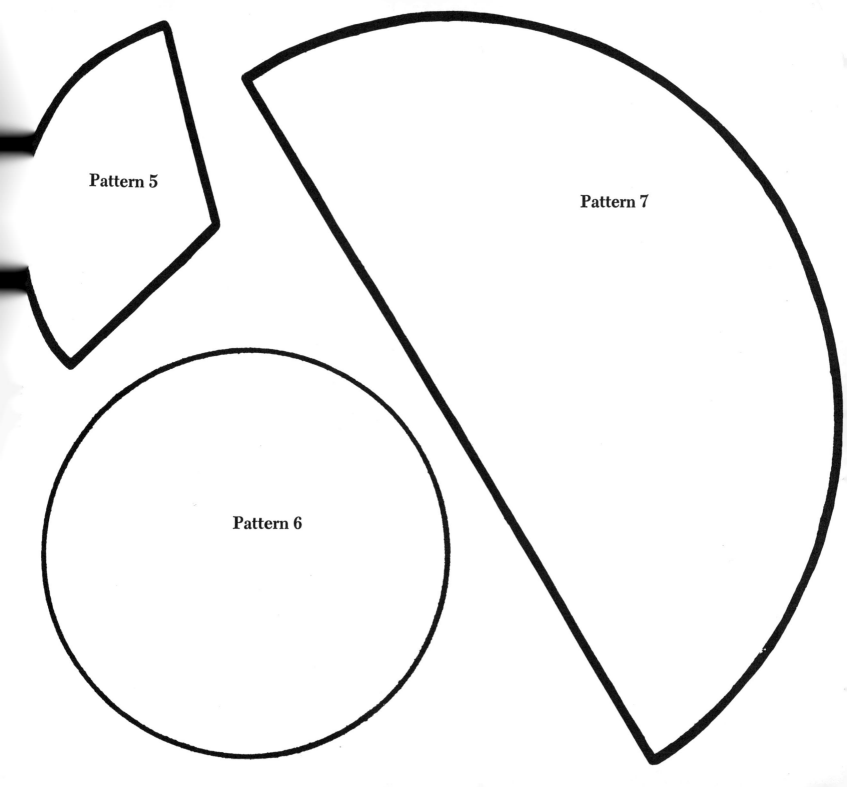

Pattern 5

Pattern 7

Pattern 6